ENCOUNTERS OF A SPIRITUAL NATURE

Stacey Jack-Jones

Ever since I can remember, even as a child, I've been able to have actual conversations with God. I've had several "minor" encounters where God would have spoken to me about things in my everyday life. For instance, when I was about eighteen, I went for a job interview as a telephone operator in Port of Spain. I got the job, but the interviewer told me to take a list of the persons and their extensions with which to familiarize myself before I started the following week. However, I forgot to take the list when I was leaving and only remembered when I got back to the main road, I told myself that I would not go back for it because it was too far to walk. As I was standing there, I kept hearing the Lord (though I didn't realise it was God's voice at the time), telling me to go back for the list but I stood there debating with "myself" for a while about going back or not. Finally, I could ignore the prompt to return for the list no more, so I went back for it. Not more than ten minutes after I left and returned to the main road with the list, I saw a truck carrying a twenty-foot container, overturned on the exact spot where I was standing moments before. I was absolutely shocked, knowing that if I had not moved, that truck would have been right on top of me. That is when I realised that it was actually the voice of God prompting me to go back for the list.

I've had many such instances of hearing the voice of God leading me away from danger. sometimes I saw what the danger would have been if I had not obeyed and sometimes I didn't.

The encounters that I'm about to share however, are actual encounters with the spirit world and not just hearing God's voice. Some of these encounters were in dreams, some were in prayer or worship and some were when I was wide awake.

When I was sixteen, I gave my life to Christ Jesus. I was baptised and started attending church. However, I did not attend bible study or prayer meetings, I simply went to church on Sunday mornings as I did not realise how important it was to get into the Word of God (**Psalm 119:9-12; v105**) and to be joined in prayer with fellow believers (**Psalm 133, Matthew 18:1-20**), even though I loved the Lord with all my heart. Therefore, when I started working around that same time, because I was not spiritually grounded, it was easy for me to slip back into the world and I did so gradually without realising it, until I was fully backslidden. In everything that happened throughout my life though, I've always been able to maintain communication with God except for one period when I truly felt as though He had abandoned me. But even then, when I cried out and said "Jesus, you said you know how we feel in every situation because you lived as a man, but you do not know what it is to feel as though God has abandoned you!" Immediately, I heard the scripture "Eli, Eli, lama sabachthani? My God, my God, why hast thou forsaken me?" (**Matthew 27:46**). I just laughed to myself, apologized and continued on my way.

DOING ME

My first memory of a spiritual encounter was a fleeting one. Even though I was in a backslidden state, I usually still had conversations with the Lord. I operated as though He was this friend who I could tell anything to or ask anything. There was a time I was about to fall asleep but I had to wake up at a certain time to go to work. However, I was worried that I would oversleep and no one else was at home for me to request that someone wake me (I don't think that there were any alarm clocks in the house!). So, as I was falling asleep, I said "Lord, can you wake me at such a time please" (I can't remember the specific time) and I fell fast asleep. Suddenly, I felt someone touch my foot and call my name very gently. I woke up and immediately checked the time, it was the exact time that I had asked the Lord to wake me. I got up and walked around the house to see who had awakened me, but I was still the only person at home. Even though I had asked the Lord to wake me, I was absolutely amazed because the touch and the voice were so real that I almost couldn't believe it. This made me realise that God cares even about the little things in our lives (**Luke 12:6-7**).

A little while after the above incident, when I was still sixteen, I remember being by the kitchen sink washing some dishes. Ever since I was a little girl, I always had a sense that I was never alone even when I was by myself. I usually felt a presence with me all the time, not one that was malignant but one that was just watching. Just there, just observing. Sometimes the presence was so strong that I would look over my shoulder to see if someone was behind me but I would see no one. This particular day however, as I stood at the sink, out of the corner of my eye I saw a huge figure standing directly behind me, as close as possible without touching me. It had the face of an eagle with black eyes, huge wings and the body of a human, which was armoured at the chest. It kept looking all around, quickly and intently with its fierce black eyes, but when it looked back at me, its eyes were like a pool with endless depth and an unexplainable love emanating from them. Even though it was but a brief vision, I was able to glean all that I just described. In that moment, not having any real knowledge about spiritual things, I said "God, I do not believe that this being is meant to do me evil, but even if it is of You, I would prefer not to see or feel it." In that instant, I could no longer feel it or see it. Somehow, I knew that it was not taken away but that my request to not be aware of it was granted. Imagine my tremendous regret in later years, when I became more spiritually aware, and realized that I must have seen an angel standing behind me. When this realization hit, I asked God to allow me to see or feel the presence again. To date, this request has not been granted in full, as I am only able to sense its presence from time to time, especially in the midst of my worship.

Another time, when I was in my early twenties, I had a dream that seemed more like a vision. In my dream/vision, I was walking to my mother's house. Now the place where my mom lives is a bit forested with a river running alongside the roadway. As I was walking in one of the darkest areas of the road, there suddenly appeared a host of angels, dressed in white garments, hovering over the trees by the river, standing in rows like a choir, singing a song that was very familiar to me (which I remembered for a few years after that encounter but unfortunately cannot recall now). As I stood there looking at them, I felt the glory of God flowing through the entire area. When I woke up, I was scared and trembling but also confused by this fear because the experience itself was so awesome. I asked my godfather, who is a pastor, why I was so scared and he explained that in most spiritual encounters in the bible the people were afraid because the human mind cannot comprehend nor cope with spiritual things, and I'm guessing more so for me, as I was in a sinful state (Isaiah 6:5, Luke 1:11-12, Daniel 10:7-12). That experience left me shaken for a while but even so, I did not give my life back to the Lord at that time.

A few years after that encounter, I started living with my boyfriend even though I knew better. Still having regular conversations with God but no real relationship. During those years, the Lord kept calling me back to Him but I wanted to live my own life. I remember my twin cousins telling me that they were praying for my salvation and I just rolled my eyes because I was "doing me". I lived with my boyfriend for about three years, then things started to fall apart. To this day, I cannot say what actually went wrong. I just started to feel as though my life was not where it was supposed to be and I simply could not go on with that relationship. I felt lost and hopeless. However, I also felt like I could not leave even though there was absolutely nothing stopping me from leaving. I remember standing by the window one day with tears streaming down my face, my heart longing for something I could not understand and I told God that if He got me out of there, I would serve Him. Within a week of that prayer, my boyfriend and I had the worst fight of our relationship, well actually he was the one who was quite irate while I, who was usually the one that would "cuss" and carry on at the drop of a hat, was very calm. I kept telling him to calm down; to take a walk so that he could clear his head, but he continued ranting. Somehow, I just knew that this was the end of the road for us so I started packing my clothes, which I had done on one occasion before but when he asked me to stay, I did. This time again, when he realized that I started to pack my stuff, he suddenly calmed down and started apologizing but there was an unwavering determination in my mind, my heart and my spirit to leave. I couldn't live in this state for one moment more. I literally wasn't angry, I wasn't hurt, and I wasn't disturbed. **I was just done**.

I walked out of the door that day with a finality in my spirit, knowing that the relationship was over and remembering my promise to God that I would serve Him if He got me out of there. I started attending church for a while, but as human beings are wont to do, I started doing my own thing again not long after that. I used to say if I was one of the Israelites whom God delivered from Egypt, I would serve Him without any doubt. I couldn't understand how those Israelites witnessed so many miracles and still doubted God, chose to serve other gods whenever they encountered a problem or turned their backs on Him when things were good with them. The Spirit of God has since opened my eyes to see that I did the same thing that the Israelites did by turning my back on Him after He delivered me and even now, because He has delivered me from so many things, and has been there for me through so many rough times, yet sometimes when I encounter a new or even familiar "issue" I tend to worry a lot, forgetting that God saw me through before and He is well able to do it again **(Philippians 4:6-7)**. Anyhoo, I've digressed.

A few months after leaving (*actually, a better statement is "after being rescued"*), I met and "fell in love" with a guy from my job. Let's call him Sam. At the beginning of this relationship, there was some evidence that Sam was still in a relationship with the mother of his child. However, he lied like a pro and after a while, there was no longer any ready evidence of their ongoing relationship. This relationship with Sam was a lot of fun and soon I totally forgot all about my promise to God. This guy was extremely thoughtful and was willing to give me anything I asked for as well as things I didn't even ask for. About a year into our relationship, I started once again seeing evidence that I was not the only person involved in his life. I asked him about some pictures that I saw on his phone and he vehemently denied any wrongdoing, so I dismissed it. One night, not long after that, I got a phone call asking if I was his girlfriend, I said yes and the person hung up. I asked Sam about it but he shrugged it off and we moved on. Even though I kept asking over and over if he was involved with anyone else, he kept denying it with everything that he had in him. One day, we were at the beach bobbing along with the waves, just laughing and talking. I was in his arms and he looked deep into my eyes and said that we would be together like this forever. Immediately the Spirit of the Lord said "**NO**" and it was the most final thing that I've ever heard or experienced in my life. It was not a shout or even a loud voice but it was almost as though in that moment, there was no room in my mind or spirit for anything else. The "**NO**" filled my entire being and I knew then, without a doubt that it was over but I held on and continued "doing me".

It was not long after this experience that things took a turn for the worst. I got pregnant for Sam and when I told him, he said that the mother of his child was also pregnant and he asked me to "get rid of mine". Because this book is about my spiritual encounters, I will not go into the full details of this experience, however it can be found in my soon to be released book "***Overcoming Every Obstacle, To Be Who God Created Me To Be***". As may be expected, this was the last straw for our relationship. His pregnant girlfriend suddenly reappeared with threats to my life to the point where both Sam and I ended up in a courtroom as I sought a protection order against him. His girlfriend was there at every turn. Suddenly, she started dropping him off at work every day, called and threatened me and even came to my godfather's house where I was staying at the time, with the intention of fighting me. The entire situation had me so stressed that I started to feel as though I was losing my mind. I wanted to kill Sam so badly, I pictured his blood flowing from his body almost every day, but my god sister kept encouraging me to just forget about him. As the days went on, the harassment became almost intolerable. Then, one night I had a dream where Sam and his girlfriend were running after me. I knew in the dream that their express intent was to kill me. I ran and ran but they pursued me relentlessly until we came upon a deep, dark abyss. There was nowhere else to go and their faces were murderous as they thundered towards me. As I approached the abyss, I looked back again knowing that this was my end because I was either going to end up in that deep darkness with all hope lost or be taken out by their very hands. However, as I watched, coming after us was a humongous snake. The snake towered over us, with a look of pure anger on its face, and its eyes like that of fire, fixed solely upon them. This was the most beautiful snake I had ever seen. Its scales shone and sparkled from the crown of its head and along its entire upper body with jewels of different shapes and colours, that I have never seen before or after (I could not see past its upper body for its sheer size). As I continued to watch, I realized that we all looked very miniature in comparison to this snake. I also knew beyond the shadow of a doubt that the snake was not there to harm me, but just as their intention was to destroy me, so was the intent of this bejeweled serpent toward them. They were so absorbed with ensuring my demise that they did not realise that they too were being pursued. Suddenly, the snake slammed its enormous head on them both and they were instantly and totally crushed. At that moment in my "dream" I knew that the battle with Sam and his girlfriend was over. Believe it or not, but the very next day, as Sam's girlfriend dropped him off at our workplace, I felt a great peace, which replaced my anxiety and from that day onward they literally had nothing to say to me or even looked in my direction. I realized from this experience that God fights for us even in our disobedience. We may have to go through the valley of the shadow of death because of our disobedience but His rod and His staff shall surely comfort us. (**Psalm 23:4**).

WALKING
WITH
KING JESUS

After this, you would think that I ran straight into the arms of God, right? Well, I did, sort of. I was in two more short-term relationships while I was "in church" but no matter who I was with, I felt empty and hopeless so I decided to commit my life totally to God because I just could not go on without Him. I started spending time in prayer and reading my bible at every opportunity. I went directly from work to church sometimes just to spend time in prayer by myself before prayer meeting or bible study. I would wake early in the morning and worship, pray and read my bible while most of the household was still asleep. I took my bible with me everywhere I went and read it at every opportunity I got. This practice caused me to step into a different level of my relationship with God. One that was way more than just casual conversation with Him.

One of my favourite experiences from spending time in God's Word and in His presence, was when I was filled with the Holy Spirit. In bible study at the time, Pastor Cliff was teaching on the Holy Spirit and I was simply entranced. I read scriptures concerning the Holy Spirit over and over and longed to be filled and speak in other tongues. However, try as I might it was not happening. I remember being in church with the keyboardist one Friday evening before choir practice started and we began singing some worship songs and then just freestyle worshipping, when he began speaking in tongues. I said "but God, you forgot me? Look at how long I'm desiring to speak in tongues and I cannot." Still, nothing happened, so I just continued with my worship and enjoyed the presence of the Lord. I went home to my mother's house that evening with the Holy Spirit and my desire to speak with other tongues at the forefront of my mind. At about 1:30 a.m., the next morning, I woke up worshipping softly, then suddenly, tongues started pouring out of my mouth. It was as though a river was flowing out of me. Pouring, pouring, pouring out into the room. My entire being was filled and I felt warmth and joy and peace from my very hair strands, down to my toes. God's presence filled my room and I sat there worshipping for a very long time. When it was over, I lay down and felt His presence cover me like a literal blanket, and that is how I fell back asleep. Sadly though, I was telling someone from church, an elder to be exact, about how the Lord had covered me like a blanket. The person looked at me with uncertainty and a trace of fear and asked if I was sure that it was "the Lord" that I felt. I said yes and we changed the topic. However, as I walked away, my heart ached to know that it was so easy for that person to believe that it was the presence of something evil rather than the presence of God.

At one point, I was staying at my godparents' home with two of my god sisters, Shianne and Anastasis, as the rest of the family was out of the country. One of Shianne's friends, Sasha was also staying at the house with us. At about 4:30 one morning, I got up to use the bathroom. As soon as I got off the bed, I started singing a worship song while I made my way to the bathroom. As I was walking past the room where Sasha lay asleep with the door ajar, out of the corner of my eyes I saw a tall, ageable, Caucasian man with a long, full beard, a black top hat and a long, black tail coat, standing at the side of the bed, slowly reaching his hand towards Sasha. Immediately I took a step back but saw nothing. I shrugged it off as possibly my imagination and continued on my way to the bathroom. I forgot all about this incident until later in the day when Sasha, Anastasis and I were in the living room watching a movie and Sasha started telling us how she was asleep that morning and she was dreaming that a tall, ageable, Caucasian man with a long, full beard, a black top hat and a long, black tailcoat was slowly reaching his hand toward her but when I started singing, he suddenly disappeared. Well, dear reader, you can imagine my shock but I said nothing to her because I did not want to scare her.

As I continued to spend more time in God's presence, I experienced more and more of the spirit realm. One time, our church went to an indoor crusade at another church in Sangre Grande and as our Pastor raised a praise and the entire church started to praise, my eyes were initially closed, but as I opened my eyes and looked up, it was as though the roof of the church had been removed and I saw Jesus riding on a pure white horse atop a mountain of clouds. As I began to doubt what I was seeing,

I heard my pastor describing exactly what I was seeing. The moment passed as quickly as it came but I was left in awe of that experience.

There were lots of little spiritual experiences in between major ones. There was a time when Sasha decided to open a hairdressing salon, as she was very good at hairdressing. She asked Pastor Cliff to bless the place she had gotten, so Shianne and I went with them. As the four of us stood holding hands and Pastor Cliff started to pray, I saw a tall, dark-green, slimy-looking creature with long bony hands and feet, an oblong hairless head, large eyes and two small holes for a nose. It looked like what some aliens purportedly look like. As Pastor continued to pray, this creature picked up a briefcase and looked around sadly, almost in disappointment and headed towards the door. Again, as I started to doubt what I was seeing, Pastor Cliff said "that's right, you pick up your baggage and leave this place right now". The creature gave one last, aggrieved look and disappeared through the door. I was absolutely amazed by what I had just experienced but surprisingly, I was totally unafraid.

One of the scariest spiritual experiences also came when I was at my mother's house. At the time, I was back and forth between my mother's and godparent's houses but I had spent the last couple of weeks at my mother's. One night I was asleep with my back turned to the wall, which is how I usually sleep. Suddenly, I opened my eyes and saw the ceiling tiles being removed and a man climbing down into my room. This "man" was more in the form of a shadow but with substance. For lack of a better description, I'd say he was a solid shadow. As he was climbing down, he slipped and fell onto the bed between the wall and me. I instantly froze so that he would not know that I was awake. At the same time, he froze to see if he had awakened me. We both stayed like this for a few minutes. My heart was pounding, my breathing shallow. He then started sliding off the bed as quietly as possible. When he got to the end of the bed and stood up, I felt the mattress spring back as his weight was lifted off it and I saw him

walk towards the door. During this time, I had not moved a muscle. I seemed to be absolutely frozen except for the aforementioned pounding of my heart and shallowed breathing. He opened the door slowly and quietly, but as he closed it, I heard the "click" from the latch on the door and felt my physical eyes open. That is when I realized that I had not been physically awake all along. I immediately began to feel a lot more fear but I told myself that my little brother had probably come into my room for something and my dream had somehow gotten mixed with reality and caused that scenario to unfold.

Therefore, I got off my bed, opened my bedroom door which led to the kitchen and saw no one. No worries, he probably got back to his room already. The entire house was dead silent as I walked through the kitchen, through my sister's bedroom (she was fast asleep), along the corridor and into my brother's bedroom. There I found him in a deep sleep. I know this because I called out to him a couple of times and he did not stir. Everyone in the house was sound asleep. As it started to dawn on me that this was spiritual, I became absolutely terrified as I returned to my room. I got back into bed and started to pray, but it seemed as though the more I prayed the more afraid I became. I started to sing worship songs, started speaking in tongues, started quoting Psalms. Nothing worked. I felt my blood become like ice in my veins, such was the fear I experienced. After about half an hour to forty-five minutes of this, I sat up abruptly and said "the Lord has not given me a spirit of fear, but one of power, love and of a sound mind. You see me, I'm really tired and I want to sleep. You spirit, wherever you came from, go from here in the name of Jesus because I am not afraid of you." Immediately after saying this, I fell into a wonderful sleep and did not wake again until morning.

When I woke up the next morning, I had a feeling that I knew who had come into my room. There was a guy who lived up the hill from my mom and he worked in the same vicinity as me. I saw him waiting for transportation one morning and decided to give him a lift to the corner. However, I ended up I taking him straight to his workplace as I had to pass there on my way to work. After that morning, he put himself in place every morning for a few weeks to get a lift. I thought nothing of it at the time, but just saw it as someone who was happy to save transportation money by waiting for a lift. However, the morning after my experience, I got a very strong feeling that he was the "person" in my room the night before but because I try not to be accusatory and usually give people the benefit of the doubt, I said "Lord, if he is the person/spirit that was in my room last night, I don't want him to ever set foot in my vehicle again." Dear readers, this guy never waited to get a lift from me from that day forward. I truly believe that he practiced/practices astral projection.

Following the last episode, I had several minor run-ins with spirits, some of which I can't fully remember. However, one of the most memorable ones to happen after that was one night while I was asleep, I felt the bed compress and at the same time I saw in the spirit world, a very small, furry animal-like creature jump onto the edge of my bed. At that point in time, I was so filled with the Holy Spirit that I was not even afraid. I simply told the thing to get off my bed and out of my room in the name of Jesus. It immediately jumped back off the bed and went through the door and I went back to a peaceful sleep.

Notwithstanding all that I spoke about before, one of my most awesome experiences within the spiritual realm came while I was at church one day. We were in the midst of our worship service and I was standing in the front at my usual spot. I cannot recall the song that was being sung at the time but in the middle of that song, I remember lifting my hands while my eyes were closed and I said "Lord, take me higher". Immediately, I felt my spirit leave my body and I ended up in what, in my mind, was the throne room of God. In this place, as far as my eyes could see, were people in pure white garments dancing, singing and rejoicing. The atmosphere was one of pure joy and jubilation such as I had never known before. As I looked around, I saw a gigantic throne with something that looked like fog rolling off it. In the midst of the fog, was a figure that filled the entire throne. As I watched in awe, I realized that I was able to see the form of this person but no specific features. It felt like a long time that I was there dancing and singing along with everyone else but after a while I opened my eyes and found myself back in church and the same song was being sung. As I readjusted to being back in church, feeling the excitement and exuberance of what had just happened, I heard a voice saying "That was not possible, it was all in your mind". As soon as I heard this voice, the lady standing next to me exclaimed "Wow! I was just in the throne room of God" and she went on to describe all that I had just seen and experienced. I couldn't help but laugh at the fact that the devil had tried to steal my experience from me by making me believe that I had imagined the entire thing, but God counteracted immediately by having the lady describe the very same experience, thereby confirming for me that what had just happened was so real.

Sometime after this encounter, I was laying on my bed a little while after coming home from church. My brother's wife called out to me and said that he wanted me to take him to the hospital as he was not feeling well. While I was getting dressed, the Lord told me to go and touch him and command him to be healed in the name of Jesus. I immediately felt an immense heat coursing through my hands at the Lord's command. However, as I left my bedroom to go to his and do as the Lord said, I became afraid and decided that I wouldn't do it. My reasoning was "maybe it won't work". As soon as I made that decision, just as quickly as my hands became hot, the heat left my hands. I then took my brother to the hospital. I've really regretted not following through with God's command that day.

All of the above-mentioned experiences took place before I was married and was living either with my mom or with my godparents. However, a few years after I got married, my husband, our three-year-old child and I moved to Sangre Grande (I was at a very early stage in my second pregnancy). On one side of the house that we were renting, there was a decrepit, abandoned house, overgrown with bushes. On the other side of our house lived a short, fat, bald headed, light skinned, old man of East Indian descent. When we moved in, he came over and introduced himself as "Bubba". He chatted with us a bit and told us that he was the one maintaining the yard for the owner before we moved in and if it was ok with us, he could continue to do so. The backyard was basically dirt/mud, so wild bush grew freely and as such, required regular maintenance. We told him that we would let him know if we needed him to continue.

From the moment we met Bubba I felt a sense of discomfort. However, I didn't actually see anything off and when I asked my husband about it, he said he didn't see or feel anything off about the man. As I am not really a very social person, I attributed my discomfort to this and moved on. However, over time that sense of discomfort concerning Bubba did not go away so I decided to just pray and cover my family against anything that he may have had intentions of doing. Because my husband is very social, he grew a bit close with Bubba even though I advised him against it. Something just was not feeling right. Maybe it was just the way he smiled when he saw me or how it seemed as though he was always watching. Not in a sexual way but just always watching us.

Bubba had a white dog with brown spots that was always in front of his door or lying on the driveway. There was also a "friend" of his who came EVERY SINGLE DAY. I do not know if I ever knew his name and even if I did, I cannot recall it at this time. He was a tall man of African descent, who was dark brown in complexion but otherwise very nondescript. He would reach Bubba's house around three or four o'clock in the afternoon and stay until the wee hours of the morning before leaving and returning later in the afternoon.

There were times when I would wake up around 4 a.m. and go into the living room to pray. Bubba's door would always be open at that time, with the dog lying around and his friend sitting somewhere within view. This seemed very odd to me and one day the Holy Spirit told me to get up at 3 a.m. instead to pray. As I obeyed the Holy Spirit and began getting up earlier over the next few days, I realized that his door was no longer open at that hour and no one was sitting outside.

After this, the first of many encounters started. One evening, I was in the kitchen making dinner. Now, the kitchen door opened unto the previously-mentioned abandoned house. I was usually not afraid of having the door opened at that hour even though the house was overgrown with bushes and the area was quite dark. However, that evening I felt a sudden sense of fear as I was preparing my meal. I looked outside and saw nothing but felt goosebumps all over my body. As the fear persisted, I felt an urgency to close the door but I shrugged it off and continued what I was doing. A few moments after this, my son came into the kitchen and stared straight at the doorway with a look of fear plastered over his tiny face. His only words were "mummy, can you close the door please?" I waited for nothing else and immediately closed the door.

A few months before my second son was born, I had a dream where I saw Bubba's tall friend standing at the foot of the bed where my husband and I were asleep. He was staring directly at me. Before I knew it, Bubba appeared next to him and said "I told you to take the baby, what are you waiting for?" However, the man seemed scared and did not move even though Bubba continued to berate him. Bubba, who was visibly upset, said that he would do it himself and proceeded to stretch his hand toward me. As I saw him approaching, I yelled "You Will Not Take My Baby In The Name of JESUS!" As I said this, they both disappeared and I woke up. I prayed over my unborn child, my son and husband who were still fast asleep and over the entire house, then resumed my sleep.

When it was time for me to have the baby, my husband took me to the hospital and returned home with our son as husbands are not allowed in the labour room at that particular hospital. I got there at about 4 a.m. and was ready to deliver by 8 a.m. There was one particular nurse that morning who was extremely nice to me, however her shift ended at the very moment that my water broke. She said that she would've liked to stay and see me through but that she really needed to leave. I told her that it was ok because my experience with my first son at a different hospital was quick and easy so I was expecting the same at this time. I should mention that whenever I am going anywhere, I pray for favour. It could be the bank, a school, a government office, hospital etc. However, when the nurse that I mentioned before left, the nurse who took over immediately started treating me in a very rough manner. She was no help at all. Any question or concern directed to her was met with a very obnoxious response. She was literally being abrasive for no apparent reason. So, I kept quiet in my pain for the most part and continuously prayed in my mind.

As I began to go into full labour, this nurse kept me in a diaper that she had me put on before and then proceeded to write in a notebook without looking up or saying anything except to tell me every few moments not to push. Meanwhile, another nurse along with a student nurse were standing by the side of the bed. The student nurse looked rather disturbed about the entire scenario but the other nurse looked as though she was not even in the room. The room felt still and almost as though time had stopped. As my contractions became stronger, I felt the baby coming and I told the nurse that the baby's head is almost out. As I said this, it was as though something snapped and the nurse in charge, who was writing in her book all along, started moving quickly and shouting in my direction to remove the diaper (I'm not sure whether she was speaking to me or one of the other nurses). All the while I had been praying silently. As soon as the diaper was removed, the baby came out and the same nurse who was so hostile from the beginning, became the nicest person. I could not believe it. After I was taken back to my bed with the baby, the student nurse, came and spoke with me. She said that she could not believe what was happening in there and that it was definitely not normal procedure. We discussed it a bit and then she left. I don't think I saw her for the next couple of days that I was at the hospital before being discharged. To this day, I truly believe that it was a spiritual attack designed to take the life of the baby.

After going home from the hospital, things were quiet spiritually for a few months, or so it seemed. One evening, when the baby was about four months old, I came home with the two children. My husband was still at work, so as I usually did, I got out of the vehicle, which was parked directly in front of the door and opened the front door to take the children inside. The older one was asleep and the baby was awake. However, as I opened the door and peeked inside, I saw the living room wall covered with ticks. I was totally shocked and disgusted. Upon closer inspection, I realized that there were ticks covering two walls as well as one of the couches. My blood was absolutely crawling. I wanted to throw up. My first instinct was to get back in the car and drive back to Maloney to wait for my husband but that would've been a long drive and he was working late that night. So, I pulled myself together because the children were still in the car, opened the back door of the house, got them out of the car and took them to their bedroom. With a screaming baby in the bedroom, I returned to the living room to deal with the disgusting scenario. I took a tin of bug spray and started spraying like crazy. There were big ones, medium sized ones and babies. They started falling off the walls as I sprayed and tried to keep the bile from rising. When I was finished, I opened the door to sweep them out and get rid of the bug spray scent. As I opened the door and looked up, I saw Bubba sitting with another neighbor in her yard directly across from me. They were both looking at me intently. Bubba had a smirk on his face. I said nothing and went back inside.

The next day, the same thing happened, I walked into the living room and there were ticks on the wall. Not as much as the day before, but one would've been too much for me. I repeated my actions of the day before. However, this time I started looking for the source of this repulsive invasion. I truly cannot recall if it was the Holy Spirit who told me where to look or if I just happened to look there, but when I looked in the corner of the window sill, there buried deep down inside, lay a large tick, full of blood. You can imagine my horror (nausea is my friend even now, writing about it). I looked on the other side of the window sill. Same thing! It took every ounce of my mental strength to take a hairpin and remove those two ticks. I carried them outside and crushed them with a stone. Bubba was in his yard watching!

For a while after this incident, things were quiet spiritually. However, a couple of months later, I dreamt that Bubba and my husband were in the backyard. They were discussing planting some trees there and I was trying to signal to my husband that I did not want Bubba planting anything in the yard. However, he seemed totally unaware that I was trying to get his attention. Bubba on the other hand, looked at me and smiled a malevolent-looking smile. It was as though he was saying "I've got you now." At that moment in my dream, I looked directly at him and said "You want to play with me? **I will kill your dog!**" I have absolutely no idea why I told him that but as soon as those words left my mouth, the blood drained from Bubba's face and he looked stricken. It was as though he felt those words deep within his very being. The dream ended and I woke up and began to pray.

During that same week, with my dream being the furthest thing from my mind, to my great astonishment, Bubba's tall friend drove his van into the driveway and accidentally rolled over Bubba's dog. Guess what! It died...

With the new baby and a three-year-old, things were really hectic, so my prayer life started to take a hit. However, it's a good thing that we have a God who understands every situation and every timeline in our lives, so while I may have been unable to spend the amount of time in prayer and reading of the Word like I used to, I was able to maintain my spiritual connection to God just by getting in a few minutes with Him throughout the day whenever I could.

After Bubba's dog died, there were no attacks for a long time. However, one night I was home alone with the kids and after putting them to bed, I went into the other bedroom to continue with some chores. No sooner was I in the bedroom, than it sounded as though the galvanize on the roof started to move. The more I heard the galvanize moving, the more I felt the coldness of fear start creeping into my being. In just a few moments, I was so afraid that I went onto the bed and curled up into a fetal position. I was literally unable to move from this position because the fear had gripped me so strongly. But when, in one clear moment, I thought about my children sleeping in the other room with whatever it was that was trying to come through the roof, I uncurled myself from that position, got off the bed and said "whatever you are, I command you to leave and do not come back in the name of Jesus". As soon as I said that, I felt the grip of fear leave me and the sounds stopped coming from the roof. I then went about my business for the rest of the night until I was ready to sleep and that was the end of that.

A little while after this last event, the Lord told me that He was going to move me. I actually thought that He was going to allow me to be transferred from my department at work in order to be closer to home because at the time, the commute from home to work and back was exhausting due to the distance. However, our landlady called shortly thereafter and said that she needed to move into the house so that her daughter could be closer to school, therefore we had to move out in a couple of weeks. The Lord then moved us to an apartment in Arima, where the landlords are an older couple who have a personal relationship with Him.

After moving to Arima, one Sunday when church was over, a group of us decided to go to the beach. We went to a sort of secluded beach and enjoyed ourselves for a few hours. When it was time to leave, everyone started walking to the area where we were parked. However, I decided to go back into the water to fill a bottle in order to wash my feet before getting into the car, as there was no pipe borne water in sight. As I entered the water, I felt a bit uneasy when I bent to fill the bottle. However, because I grew up hearing that "you must not go back into the water for "one last dip" after everyone decides to leave because that's how most people drown", I at first passed the feeling off as me remembering that saying, even though I did not actually go back for a last dip. Within a few seconds though, that "bit" of uneasiness turned into a sense of total dread, as I had a sense that something terrible was coming towards me from under the water at a phenomenal speed. This "thing" felt powerful and as though it encompassed the entire area where we were. I started repeating the name of Jesus, while willing the bottle to fill quickly. As soon as I had enough water I hurried out of the sea and went to where Anastasis was waiting for me. I said "Ana, you would not believe what just happened." I related what had happened and told her that I don't understand why I got that feeling. She suggested that we do not linger any more, as most of the group was already further up the hill. As we were walking to meet up with the group, we saw a lady who was known to us from our school days. She was dressed in a long, full, pleated skirt, a fitted bodice and a head wrap and had a container in her hand with what seemed to be milk or some type of white liquid. We greeted her and asked what she was doing there and she replied that she now lived just up the road. She gestured to the container in her hand and said that she was going down to the sea to offer up its contents. Anastasis and I looked at each other, bade the lady goodbye and moved quickly towards our vehicle as we understood that the "thing" that I felt coming, was actually coming to receive her offerings.

Strangely, I had a similar experience a few years later when Anastasis and I were visiting her sister in the U.S.A. Now, Makeda's home is located in a lovely suburban area, where the houses are surrounded by huge trees and there are no streetlights, so the nights are pitch black. I usually love these types of settings, so neither the placidity of the day nor the utter darkness of the night, bothers me. One night, Makeda's husband stayed in the city as he had to conduct some business early the next day, so the three of us watched a movie and then I retired to bed around ten o'clock. Anastasis and Makeda, who are both night owls, stayed up watching movies and talking. At about two a.m., the Lord woke me up and I heard Makeda moving around in the kitchen. The Lord told me to go and pray with her, but I was really tired and wanted to continue sleeping so I told the Lord that I would pray with her later in the morning when we woke up. I started to fall back asleep but the Lord prompted me again to go pray with her. I told the Lord that I would go in a few minutes and started falling asleep again. Suddenly, I became aware that Makeda was preparing for bed and I began to panic knowing that I had not done as the Lord told me to. I jumped off the bed and said to her "Makeda, let us pray." She said OK and told me that Anastasis had suggested that we pray earlier but then they decided to wait until later in the morning. I told her that the Lord said to pray now, so she woke Anastasis. As we began to pray, I sensed a terrifying power coming in our direction at lightning speed and it seemed as though it encompassed the entire area. However, as we continued to pray in earnest, calling on the name of Jesus, the "power" fell back and dissipated altogether. After that, we remained in prayer for a while, then went to sleep.

The last entry that I will place into this book, happened after the Lord moved us to Arima, which is where we live at the writing of said book. One morning, I did not go to work for some reason. After the children left for school and my husband left for work, I went back to sleep. As I was sleeping, I dreamt that I woke up and started to move around the house. After a while, in my dream I realized that I was still asleep so I told myself that I would now wake up. I woke up and started moving around the house until I realized again that I was still asleep. Again, I told myself that I would just wake up. This happened about five times until I started to panic in my sleep, because I was watching myself sleeping and trying to wake up but I was unable to do so. At one point, I actually spoke sternly to myself saying "Stacey! This is a dream, all you have to do is wake up!" Yet, I was unable to do so. The final time that I lay back down in my dream, I picked up my phone and called a friend from church who lives close to us. I quickly explained to her what was happening and that I needed her to come and wake me. I told her that the back door was unlocked so she needed to pass through the back and come quickly and wake me because I had been trying to wake up for the longest while and I could not get out of my sleep. As I was trying to explain exactly what was happening, my fingers suddenly became numb and useless while holding the phone and it fell out of my hand so that I could not continue the conversation with her. I began having a full-on panic attack, felt my breathing becoming strangled and my chest beginning to constrict. I felt as though I was spiraling into someplace that I did not know. At that moment I shouted "Look here! I command you to release me in the name of Jesus!" Instantly, at those words, I came out of the dream and it took me a second or two to confirm that I was actually awake and not continuing in the loop. I got off the bed and started to pray.

Through all of my experiences, whether asleep or awake, I **KNOW** beyond the shadow of a doubt that the name of Jesus is powerful. It is higher than any other name and when we call upon that name, we are sure to be delivered from whatever the situation may be.

I **KNOW** that if God is for us, then no one can be against us.

I **KNOW** that God cares for us, in our good times and bad times, even when we turn away from Him. He doesn't like our sin but He still cares for us.

I **KNOW** that if it was not for the Lord, I would not be here today to write about my experiences.

And I **KNOW** that if you give Him a chance, He will save you, deliver you, fight for you, lift you up, set you free and love you like no other love that you've ever had or will ever experience.

I love the Lord Jesus with all my heart... Be encouraged beloved.

Made in the USA
Middletown, DE
20 August 2023

36980820R00018